Wall of Sound

Wall of Sound

Poems by

David Stephenson

© 2022 David Stephenson. All rights reserved.
This material may not be reproduced in any form, published,
reprinted, recorded, performed, broadcast,
rewritten or redistributed without
the explicit permission of David Stephenson.
All such actions are strictly prohibited by law.

Cover design by Shay Culligan
Cover image by Jean Wimmerlin

ISBN: 978-1-63980-213-5

Kelsay Books
502 South 1040 East, A-119
American Fork, Utah 84003
Kelsaybooks.com

In memory of my brother, William Dale Stephenson, and my father, Lawrence Aaron Stephenson. In coelo quies.

Acknowledgments

All of these poems have appeared previously, in one form or another, in the following publications:

14 by 14: "Gideon Bible"
Able Muse: "Lincoln Barber College"
Alabama Literary Review: "Wiring Simplified"
Angle: "Biting the Hand"
Autumn Sky Poetry: "Ex Organ Donor," "Over the Edge"
Avatar Review: "Cave Painter," "Reverse Bird Watching"
Blue Unicorn: "Cave Fish," "Free Seminar," "Paint Factory Fire," "Rainmaker," "Safecracker," "Salesman," "Toolmaker"
The Deronda Review: "At Thebes"
Extreme Sonnets: "Crop Duster," "Daredevil," "Horoscope;" reprints of "Biting the Hand," "Over the Edge," "Starlight, Star Bright"
Extreme Sonnets II: reprints of "Free Seminar," "Insect Collector"
Extreme Formal Poems: "Playing on Alone;" reprints of "Cave Painter," "Cornfields," "Lab Rat," "Mission Statement," "Snow Globe," "Voyager 2"
The Lyric: "Bombs Away," "Cornfields," "Music Lesson," "Quo Vadis, Bigfoot?" "Snow Globe," "Starlight, Star Bright," "Welder"
Measure: "Knife Grinder," "Matchbook," "Spartacus," "Strange Songs"
The Orchards Poetry Journal: "Combine," "Mission Statement," "Time Capsule"
The Raintown Review: "Frankenstein"
Slant: "Flossie," "Hospital," "Lab Rat," "Merlin," "Newton," "Palm Sunday," "Rock Quarry," "Voyager 2"
Snakeskin: "Casino," "Continuous Improvement," "Foolers," "Implosion," "Insect Collector," "Oil Change," "Police Impound Lot," "The Road Taken," "Through the Splintered Door," "Urban Farmers"
Umbrella: "Daylight Saving Time," "Homo Erectus," "Man of Steel," "Revival"

Contents

1. Brass Tacks

Time Capsule	15
Biting the Hand	16
Salesman	17
Gideon Bible	18
Homo Erectus	19
Strange Songs	20
Free Seminar	21
Knife Grinder	22
Spartacus	23
At Thebes	24
Starlight, Star Bright	25
Daylight Saving Time	26
Bombs Away	27

2. Spilled Milk

Man of Steel	31
Palm Sunday	33
Police Impound Lot	35
Paint Factory Fire	36
Urban Farmers	37
Continuous Improvement	38
Oil Change	39
The Road Taken	40
Implosion	41
Casino	42
Hospital	43
Revival	45

3. Times Past

Through the Splintered Door	49
Lincoln Barber College	50
Wiring Simplified	51
Rock Quarry	53
Foolers	54
Cornfields	55
Music Lesson	56
Combine	57

4. More Brass

Playing on Alone	61
Snow Globe	62
Horoscope	63
Crop Duster	64
Over the Edge	65
Quo Vadis, Bigfoot?	66
Insect Collector	67
Daredevil	68
Ex Organ Donor	69
Mission Statement	70
Welder	71

5. Smoke and Stone

Matchbook	75
Frankenstein	76
Lab Rat	77
Cave Fish	78
Flossie	79
Rainmaker	81
Toolmaker	82
Safecracker	83
Reverse Bird Watching	84
Merlin	85
Newton	87
Cave Painter	89
Voyager 2	91

1. Brass Tacks

Time Capsule

I plan to bury one in the old park
That's always empty, so no one will care,
Beneath a bogus homemade plaque to mark
The fake past date it wasn't interred there.

Inside I'll put a wrestling magazine,
A pack of cigarettes, a can of beer,
An old cell phone, a jar of gasoline,
And two beef jerky strips in Tupperware.

If anyone digs it up decades hence
I doubt they'll get much joy from their new haul,
Since its expertly curated contents
Won't help them understand our times at all,

Which is the point, if there is one, because
Nobody living through them right now does.

Biting the Hand

Master is the one who gives me food
From little cans or out of the big bag,
And all he seems to want is gratitude,
To hear me whimper and watch my tail wag.

Master has a tempting, meaty hand
With plump fingers and greasy fingertips
That point and wiggle with each barked command
And smell like pizza and potato chips.

I want to bite it, badly, but I can't.
No. Bad dog. I could lose everything,
My free meals, my whole living arrangement,
Just for one quick nip, to hear him sing.

Somewhere an old wolf howls on a wild hill.
I know the day is coming when I will.

Salesman

We report out monthly to the team,
So you don't have to wonder where you stand.
If you've had bookings, let's say sixty grand,
Then you're a sales machine and reign supreme;
If, however, business has been lean
And you have spent the whole month pounding sand
And tiptoe in with nothing in your hand
Then they quit celebrating and turn mean.

So I can be a hero or a bum
Based on my job's inherent ebb and flow.
It's been half each over the long haul.
When they start snarling at me, I go numb
And focus on my paycheck, since I know
It's only real life, nothing personal.

Gideon Bible

At a Ramada Inn where the TV
Was broken, fishing through the nightstand drawer,
I found a King James Bible dutifully
Placed by the Gideons, whoever they are.
It had a useful index in the front
With entries like COURAGE in Time of FEAR,
COMFORT in Time of SORROW, and some blunt
Death stuff. I kept it for a souvenir
And still read it sometimes when I'm up late.

If I ever meet a Gideon
I'll tell her that I think it's really great
That they leave all those books for everyone,
Then ask her if they have one listing out
Some passages for FAITH in Time of DOUBT.

Homo Erectus

Assembled out of fragments, the old face,
All eye-sockets and teeth and empty space,
Peers from the book I got for Father's Day,
The Evolution of the Human Race.

Was it really human? Hard to say,
Since skeletal remains do not betray
The inner life, the mind within the skull,
Where man-or-beast distinctions come in play.

You can't tell if it loved, was merciful,
Hoped, dreamed, forgave, or thought it had a soul,
If it in fact was even self-aware
From evidence so geological,

Though if you focus on its hollow stare
You can convince yourself you see despair.

Strange Songs

I don't remember how it came my way
But I have an old, umpteenth-hand CD
Of songs in a language unknown to me.
It has some fancy flute and fiddle play,
Sticks clacking and a drum thumping away,
And a woman singing soulfully,
As if to herself, enchantingly.
I listen to it almost every day.

Depending on my mood, I think she sings
Of love, or loss, or longing, or a dream.
Whatever she's saying sure sounds true.
I doubt it would take much inquiring
To find out what the songs actually mean,
But how would they be better if I knew?

Free Seminar

I use the same rote pitch night after night
To sell my real estate conversion scheme:
Charts and graphs to prove the time is right
And a healthy dose of Dare to Dream.

It's the same crowd every night as well,
Nametags, folders, coffee cups, and smiles,
Nodding as they fall under the spell,
Lingering like old friends in the aisles.

Whatever they might think they're paying for
What I sell is hope, a sure-fire way
To get in on a dangling big score.
And they feel joy imagining the day,

So on the value side, they do get some
For all the money they are parted from.

Knife Grinder

I roam the Duchy with my wheel and mule.
When I come to a settlement, I shout,
"Dull knives sharpened, axes, sickles, tools,"
And the villagers come pouring out
And form a line, each with an arsenal
Of blades to cut, carve, whittle, chop, and slice,
All nicked up, bent, corroded, and worn dull
Through the vicissitudes of village life.

They seem like simple, forthright peasant folk,
But the state of their cutlery betrays
An underside I'd rather not provoke,
So I let them pay what and when they may.
I live on little gold with little fear;
Times are often lean, but I'm still here.

Spartacus

A captive and a slave, I might have died
In the arena. But we overcame
Our guards, and took their weapons, and became
An army, plundering the countryside
And freeing slaves, and wounding Roman pride.
And so they called four legions back from Spain,
Who crushed us in a businesslike campaign.
All those they did not kill were crucified.

The Romans will record their victory.
May future slaves read through their dreary list
Of generals, battles won, and numbers slain,
And understand that we were briefly free,
And cast themselves in daydreams in our midst,
And stir at the mere mention of my name.

At Thebes

We strain at ropes to drag great blocks of stone
Up winding ramps at Pharaoh's rising tomb,
A labor which has been the grinding doom
Of thousands since he first took up his throne.
We build for Pharaoh's afterlife alone,
To seal his mummy in a secret room
With all his treasure, ready to assume
His new life in the world beyond our own.

When we die we are cast into the sand,
Forgotten, vanished into nothingness.
It is an empty, hopeless destiny,
And all the older royal tombs that stand
In lonely clumps across this wilderness
Have never awed, but only saddened me.

Starlight, Star Bright

When I gaze at the sky on a clear night
I know that all those twinkling points of light
Are dime-a-dozen suns like ours, a sea
Of other worlds extending out of sight.

I pick one out and think how it might be,
A giant gas ball burning blindingly
As unimagined planets float nearby,
Each one a snowflake of geology,

A thought of God. Observed from its strange sky
Our modest sun would hardly catch the eye
Of anyone there picking her own star
To ponder, wish upon, or reckon by,

To conjure in brief visions from afar,
To notice out of all the stars there are.

Daylight Saving Time

I own eight or nine clocks, plus a watch.
It bothers me when they don't all agree,
So I adjust them constantly, to match
Their readings, at least temporarily.

And when I almost get them all dialed in
They pull this nonsense, spring forward, fall back,
And I have to reset them all again
And they all get completely out of whack.

As hobbies go, it is a bitter cup,
This twisting knobs and dials to calibrate
Some moving targets, setting myself up
For being toyed with by the hand of fate,

Like that old Greek guy pushing on his rock.
And time keeps gushing by, tick tock, tick tock.

Bombs Away

When the moment happens, things occur
Of their own will, without warning or thought.
Lights start flashing, mechanisms stir,
And you are either ready or you're not.

All the special charges in your care,
The things you've worried over and about,
Lie in their cradles, hopefully prepared.
The trapdoor opens and they tumble out

And turn nose downward and float out of sight
Through smoke and spotlights. And you cannot know
What path they'll follow, thither in the night,
Or what will really happen far below

When circumstance puts each one to the test.
All that's left is hoping for the best.

2. Spilled Milk

Man of Steel

I was in the steel business long ago,
Rolling coils of autobody sheet
With special textured rollers, to impart
A finish which would yield a good paint job.

Our plant was a straight line of separate shops
Which stretched from ore crushers and coke ovens
To the stately, smoke-wreathed open hearth
To slab casters which molded glowing chunks

Of newborn steel, to hot mills which rolled plate,
To cold mills which reduced the plate to sheet,
To serpentine annealing furnaces,
And finally to our humble skin pass mill.

One day, as we were rolling right along,
There was a gap in coil deliveries
For hours, it seemed. We stood around like fools
Until the system got in gear again.

We soon heard rumors that the cause had been
An accident up by the open hearth;
A gas pipe fitter, high up in the roof,
Had slipped and dropped into the caster sprue

While they were pouring steel, and vaporized
In a brief hiss and telltale plume of mist.
The slab he went into had to be scrapped
For being out of spec for calcium.

A lot has changed since then. The plant is closed
But not torn down, just left to rust and rot,
The town, what's left of it, has gone to seed,
And I've quit wasting time on memories;

But I still think about that man of steel
Whose name I never heard, who fell that day
From this world to the next, and vanished in
A puff of smoke, and hardly left a trace.

Palm Sunday

The Archbishop was wearing sunglasses
And his chess-piece hat as he blessed the palms
And led the opening prayer for the few souls
Assembled in the windswept courtyard of
The stone cathedral built in richer times.

They went inside and scattered through the pews.
The Archbishop read through Mark's version of
The trial and death of Jesus, the terse tale
Of Roman frontier justice acted out
One tragic day two thousand years ago.

Like every year, the congregants were moved,
As if they heard the hammer strike the nail,
The scourge cut through the air, the timbers groan
When hoisted into place, the sudden cries
Of pain, and the cruel jeering of the crowd.

Why has this sad story from an age
Before brutality was mechanized
Remained so central to so many lives,
When all the intervening wars and kings,
The causes died for, are now meaningless?

This tale of powers aligned and doom brought down
Upon a carpenter who preached of peace
And loved those no one else loved, and who faced
The ruthless rulers of his time and place
With silence and serene indifference?

You can debate if there's a God or not,
But leaving that aside, there is a church
To preach the soothing faith of Roman slaves,
Which promises relief from worldly cares
And forgiveness, which most people want,

Forgiveness for the things that we have done
Or not done, for the people we have hurt,
For all the wreckage we have left behind,
For all the things that keep us up at night,
For all the things we wish we could make right.

The church will be here at the end of things,
When all the factories have been shut down
And all those jobs are gone, and half the town
Is being retrained by the government
For all the wistful coming industries.

They'll light the candles and put on the mass
As if they hardly noticed any change;
Another little kingdom of this world
Had come to nothing, but the mysteries
Of sin and death and meaning still remained.

As long as people linger, some will come
To sit in stained glass silence and be told
Old stories of redemption, parables
And promises, and say familiar prayers,
And dream of great joy in a world to be.

Police Impound Lot

Amid a sea of suspect vehicles
Sat my conveyance, minus one hubcap
Gone who knows where, but otherwise unscathed
From being towed. Beneath the wiper blade
A sun-dried parking ticket hugged the glass.

The office staff did business from within
A bulletproof enclosure. They took cash
Through an elaborate lever-action drawer,
After which they did your paperwork.
You bargained with them through a microphone.

No cash, no car. They popped the drawer open
When people stepped up, but some were just there
To plead a case, some partial payment scheme,
You've got to work with me, cut me a break,
I'll lose my job, I'll end up on the street.

The staff would calmly hear the person out
And then explain that that's not how it worked
If there was continued argument
They simply flipped the microphone switch off
And waited till the person went away.

Outside, beyond the scrubland near the lot,
The scattered brush and rubble and old tires,
Worn-out buildings crowded re-patched streets
Beneath a web of poles and drooping wires,
While in the distance rose the stout concrete

Pillars of a freeway overpass,
Where an arc of guard-railed roadbed showed
Only the tops of cars as they zipped by,
Casting fleeting shadows down below
Like birds flying through a patch of sky.

Paint Factory Fire

It was a brick and wood beam structure built
By bearded men in wool coats and felt hats
With pocket watches on expensive fobs.
Its long abiding oil-based background stench
Had seeped into its porous masonry,
Which breathed a small breath like the leaves on trees.

Into this world of fumes there came a spark
And flames flared from all windows on all floors
And fed a sky-high column of dark smoke,
While paint from all the ruptured drums and vats
Mixed with the fire hose water flowing past
And swirled and gathered in a mud-brown pool.

The place was not rebuilt. There was some talk
Of an insurance fraud case, but the wreck
Was bulldozed down. Some former workers came
To see the last truckloads of rubble leave
And shake hands one last time and mark the day
When all the color went out of their world.

Urban Farmers

Flourishing among the padlocked gates
And dwindling streets with houses here and there
Within a district zoned for industry

Are amber waves of fruits and vegetables
In little gardens and a few plowed fields,
The work of pioneers from parts unknown

Come to clear and farm this wilderness,
To bring forth from the former factory soil
Healthy food for happy villagers.

New futures are predicted all the time,
Assorted modified suns coming up
Like burning tires in different brand-new dawns—

Is this the true one? Will we all end up
Growing beans and squash among the ruins
And eating mush from a communal pot?

I sure won't be joining in. At dusk
The breeze blows and the weeds and beanstalks sway
And shadows creep from scarecrows and smokestacks

And you can sense the future in the dark,
The bouquet of surprises on the way,
Drawing closer by another day.

Continuous Improvement

At work they told us to look out for ways
To speed things up or cut out steps and costs
Habitually, so we would get more lean,
Which would make us more competitive.

A central tenet of their strategy
Was *Focus on the Things You Can Control,*
Which in my case isn't all that much,
Just some grease changes and scheduling—

But if you play along and zero in
On how you can improve those small details
At least there's progress, unlike in the world.
Plus you can apply the skill at home.

Right now it is my target to improve
My closeness to my daughter ten percent
By listening, not giving her advice.
And my five-point plan is working out

And I'm much happier, and pondering
Other things I could improve myself
Just by making an effort, more or less.
I still hate my job, but it's taught me this.

Oil Change

Regarding it as an essential skill
My dad taught me the art of changing oil
By following a rigid set of steps
Picked up by chance but treated as revealed,
The way they trained him at the factory.

In the last step, you wiped the drain pan clean
And lined it with six folded paper towels
Ranged origami-style around the rim
With the grease gun and cap wrench placed on top.
It was distinctive, like a signature.

I quit changing oil some years ago
But still have a drain pan in my garage
All rigged up and festooned with paper towels.
It's wilted and bedraggled and forlorn
And I should throw it out, but haven't yet.

The Road Taken

Inside an office park cubical farm,
Three rows deep and two aisles to the right,
I saw a poem pinned to a foamboard wall
Above a stapler and some paper clips,
Which said "I took the road less travelled by
And that has made all the difference."

The nearby hallways branched and forked a lot,
But all the paths showed equal wear and tear
From heavy bureaucratic foot traffic.
I wonder if whoever tacked it up
Somehow perceived some abstruse relevance
Or wished that things had turned out differently.

Implosion

A wrecking ball will rarely draw a crowd,
But when they use explosives to implode
A good-sized building, TV trucks show up
And people gather by the safety fence
And helicopters hover overhead.

There are some desultory pops before
Initial waves of charges separate
The decks and girders, climbing floor by floor
As the structure sways beneath its weight,
Until large charges cut the posts and core

And all the pieces tumble to the ground
In sequence, folding into the fall zone
Amid a wave of cataclysmic sound
As clouds of pulverized concrete and stone
Escape in billows from the rubble mound.

And the assembled spectators erupt
In massive whistling and whooping cheers
Instinctively, as if from simple joy
At the precise and orderly collapse,
A kind of beauty anyone can see.

Casino

It's on the freeway, to accommodate
Out-of-town sharps with their fabled wealth,
But it's mostly locals weekday nights
Wandering from the parking deck to ride
The escalators down to the main floor,

Where they fan out purposefully, with some
Heading for the back tables, but most
Lining up in front of slot machines
And punching buttons, focused on the task
Like workers pulling a production shift.

But it's more like a mine than factory,
Extracting, not producing, with the twist
That the gold and silver aren't dug up
But brought in by the patrons from outside,
Donated a few coins at a time.

Either way it seems more work than play
For the rank and file at the machines;
As they cycle through their standard tasks,
Most don't smile or seem at all relaxed.
I wonder if a real mine is as sad.

Hospital

It's always been there, but it's grown a lot,
Having swallowed up its neighborhood,
Some stores and houses and a heat treat shop.
Its owners have put in new capital,
The cancer unit and the MRI,
And transport people in from miles around
To keep their assets fully utilized.

People used to travel here to work
In one or another factory,
But that need for labor has dried up.
Now people are the raw material
And processed product of an industry,
Strapped on carts and moving down the line,
All stacked up between the big machines.

It is the great circle of business life,
One thing after another, logging, furs,
Farming, manufacturing, now this,
And maybe something else in twenty years.
The world spins and the pieces shift around
As in an overgrown kaleidoscope.
It's thrilling if you don't need steady work.

At least this time around the cause is good,
Since at a working level the whole point
Is to care for others. And because
Their most advanced machines require a pool
Of population to draw patients from,
They put them in big cities, even those
Where everybody else is moving out.

And so the ailing city has become
A magnet for the sick, who funnel in
From far beyond its ramshackle expanse,

Seeking treatment for an endless stream
Of ailments, illnesses, and injuries,
Coming here, of all places on Earth,
As if to someplace holy to be healed.

Revival

They used to have them when I was a kid.
A billboard would proclaim a cryptic phrase,
Perhaps "Is Christ divided in this town?"
And cite a verse from First Corinthians;
A final line would give the time and place
Of an impending Whole Truth Tent Crusade.

There were always people who would come,
More than you'd think, whole dressed-up families,
With strings of children, cousins, neighbors, aunts,
Big study bibles, handkerchiefs, and fans,
To fill the rows of folding chairs set up
Beneath an awning in a vacant lot.

They'd have some old backwoods church music first,
Then preaching. The presiding reverend
Would tell how he had been a sinner once,
Possessed by every devil they could name,
Till Jesus saw and sent the Holy Ghost
To take control and claim him for His own.

Then people from the crowd would testify:
Lord, I was lost and weak, a slave to drink;
I had the sickness, Lord, I was afraid,
The doctors said they couldn't do a thing;
I couldn't pay my bills, Lord, I was poor;
He beat me, Lord, so hard I couldn't think;

When all my world was crumbling, Lord, who cared?
When no one else would help me, who was there?
When I was struggling beneath my load,
Stumbling blindly on an uphill road,
Who suddenly appeared to comfort me
And share my yoke and burden? None but Thee.

And then the next day it would all be gone,
With only tire tracks and trampled grass
To tell the tale. The preacher would be off
To the next town. The people would return
To where they'd come from, to the old travail
Of this world, and to loneliness, and faith.

3. Times Past

Through the Splintered Door

I peer through childhood's splintered door
And see the world that was before,
Caught in a well-worn photograph
From nineteen hundred sixty-four—

A boy, a farm, a family,
A lot of old machinery,
And everyone oblivious
To everything that was to be.

The out-of-focus boy is me,
Sulking on the periphery,
But what he saw when staring back
Is now beyond recovery,

Since I can't pour back through that door
Or bore to recollection's core
And be that jug-eared boy again,
Awaiting all that was in store—

Time runs downhill, pools on the floor,
Slips down the drain, and leaves no more
Of everything that used to be
Than a loose silt of memory.

Lincoln Barber College

The theory was the students had to cut
A fixed number of heads before they got
Their barber's license. So there was a stir
When Dad and Bill and Bob and I came through
The creaking door they'd rigged up with a bell.

The novices in the dollar seats up front
Would stand up smiling and shake out their smocks,
But Dad would steer us into the back room,
Over the hair-strewn linoleum,
To the two-dollar senior student chairs.

The choices were the Butch, a straight buzz cut,
Or the Princeton, where they left you with
A stylish forelock. Bob and I got butched
Without thought, but Bill was a Princeton man
And the possessor of a pocket comb.

The talk was mostly weather, high school sports,
Cars, farm prices, jokes, and TV shows.
They had hot rod and hunting magazines.
They always asked Dad how things were at Deere
And whether or not it was a contract year.

But there wasn't much talk driving home,
Piled in the back seat of the Pontiac,
Hee-Haw music on the radio,
The windows rolled down, scooping in the air,
The wind figuratively in our hair—

Past the high school and the Baptist church,
The cemetery and Plow-Planter Works
Looming behind fences and guard shacks,
Over the viaduct and railroad tracks,
Up the big hill and no looking back.

Wiring Simplified

When I was ten or twelve years old, my dad
Got interested in electricity
And got into the fuse box, and soon had
A plan for beefing up the circuitry.

He kept his books and magazines downstairs,
Variously stood up, stacked, and filed
On a workbench by his reading chair.
There was soon an addition to the pile,

A burnt orange booklet from the hardware store
Called *Wiring Simplified,* illustrated,
Conspicuous because of its color.
We brothers were told not to mess with it.

It had pictures of all kinds of wires
Cut open with the insulation stripped
And rubber-handled screwdrivers and pliers
And meters rigged with alligator clips

And a fold-out wiring diagram
With grids of lines connecting staggered rows
Of Greek letters and cryptic pictograms
Like hieroglyphics or a secret code.

At some point he came home with coils of wire
And metal tubing and a paper sack
That clanked when it was set down on the drier,
And after he got everything unpacked

He started measuring and marking spots,
Then plugged in his electric drill to bore
A long series of rafter holes, and got
Wood shavings in his hair and on the floor;

He sawed and filed the metal tubes and used
More tools to fit some with a metal box,
And drilled more holes and tightened lots of screws
To mount them to the posts and cinderblocks.

Then he fed wire through all the holes and pipes
Into each box, and trimmed and stripped the ends
To leave small clusters of bare copper spikes
Sticking out like fingers or whole hands.

I waited upstairs when he cut the power
To wire his circuits into the main box.
You could hear him working through the floor,
Muffled footsteps, flashlight clicks, and coughs.

When I was let back downstairs he was done.
There were plugs and switches everywhere,
Plus a four-foot pull chain shop light hung
Over his workbenches and his chair.

He showed me all the galvanized hardware,
The wires snaked through rafters overhead,
The holes all lined up, all the angles square.
I wish I could remember what he said.

Rock Quarry

There was a big pit on my grandpa's farm,
Expanded from a gully between fields.
It ramped down from one end to a flat spot
Surrounded by sheer, layered limestone walls
Carved out with steam shovels and dynamite.
Water had seeped in at the far end
And corn was planted right up to the rim.

It was a county quarry for road stone,
But it was rarely worked, then not at all,
And trees grew up and animals moved in
Among the scattered quarrying debris:
Piles of gravel and loose chunks of rock,
Plastic buckets, glass bottles, steel drums,
And scraps of hose and wire and pallet wood.

We used to play there like it was a park,
Whiling away the odd hour or two
Climbing up and down the gravel piles,
Picking through the endless trove of junk,
Throwing rocks into the seepage pond
Or at nothing. Whatever came to mind.
And that should make for wholesome memories,

But what I think of most now is the walls,
The layers laid down imperceptibly,
So many million years per foot, composed
Of skeletal remains from ancient reefs;
How there must have been fossils if we'd looked,
And how no shouts are bouncing off them now,
Since there's no road, and no one knows they're there.

Foolers

"Foolers" were the culvert-dwelling carp
That flourished in the ditches between fields.
They were not highly prized as a sport fish
Yet it was my ambition as a child

To catch one, and I squandered fruitless hours
Pestering them with a bare line and hook.
Then I conceived of bait, and tried my luck
With a half baloney slice I took

From half of my lunch sandwich, and it worked,
And I stood holding a caught fish, unsure
Of what to do with it, until my mom
Came over and told me to throw it back.

Watching as it vanished up the ditch,
I felt proud that I'd caught a real live fish,
But disappointed with the end result,
Not yet aware that most schemes fizzle out.

Cornfields

When I think of the place where I was born
I picture first, involuntarily,
A landscape overrun by fields of corn

Covering every lonesome and forlorn
Square foot accessible by machinery.
I left the rolling plains where I was born

At a tender age, and did not mourn
My vanished agri-business destiny
In the ever-growing field of corn;

I found the labor easily foresworn.
Over time I've gone less frequently
Back to the plow-cut plains where I was born,

Now only when a black suit must be worn
At the township graveyard, fittingly
Surrounded on three sides by fields of corn,

And when I hear the hotel shuttle's horn
I leave, a stranger, knowing nobody
On the rolling plains where I was born
Where all my dead lie buried in the corn.

Music Lesson

My older brother had a record player,
So I learned music through the bedroom wall,
A muffled three-chord rumble jiggling all
Loose objects in my shared abutting lair
And wafting from his closed door down the hall.

I liked what I heard, and over years
We discussed and analyzed new bands,
With speed and volume being our main demands.
There was always new music to hear.
Then came endless silence on his end.

Now when I hear some long-lost favorite song,
Dragging its kite tail of memory,
I still feel the joy and energy,
But also the past whispering along
Within the rhythm and the melody.

Combine

It wasn't like the big ones they have now,
All self-propelled. You dragged this one behind
A tractor, and its three-row scissor head
Chopped the corn stalks, and its box frame shook,
And shelled corn trickled out of a side chute,
And mangled stalks and cobs out the back end.

It was a "combine" because it combined
Reaping and threshing, which are separate trades
In the Bible, plied with scythes and flails.
It was the flagship of a little fleet,
Escorted by a wagon as it went
About its fateful business in the fields.

As with anything, when it broke down
They dragged it to the barnyard and began
Disassembling it. My grandpa used
Pliers to loosen bolts, and Dad would say
That maybe he should try a normal wrench
Instead of chewing up the heads like that.

After they removed some sheet metal
One of them would crouch and reach inside,
Twisting and contorting as required,
While the other passed him different tools,
Until at length a greasy arm emerged
Holding something twisted, snapped, or seized.

Looking at its uncovered details,
The dense array of shafts and linkages,
I wondered how they knew how it all worked,
What could go wrong and where they should look,
How they always found the broken part
And how I'd ever learn to be that smart.

4. More Brass

Playing on Alone

A band I once saw in the distant past
Toured through my town, and I went to the show,
Figuring this tour would be their last
Since they should have quit playing years ago.

The act was just the old band's lead guitar
With rent-a-rockers on the drums and bass,
Performing in a storefront with a bar
But no seating, just empty standing space.

As I watched that old timer cycle through
Forgotten hits for microscopic pay
In that obscure and pitiful venue
I felt sad that he'd ended up that way,

Until I noticed that he didn't care,
But looked relaxed and in his element,
Despite the small crowd and old friends not there—
Absorbed in song and seemingly content

To just make music, as a daily goal,
As long as someone came to hear him play,
A lot more for the soul than the bankroll.
I went home wishing I could live that way.

Snow Globe

Beneath a two-piece plastic clamshell dome
With painted sunbeams and a trapped air bubble,
Some friendly flattened people make their home.
Heavy snowstorms cause them endless trouble,

Since periodically their whole world shakes
And their sloshing, liquid atmosphere
Fills up with swarms of basketball-sized flakes
Which fall and drift, but never disappear,

Half burying their not-to-scale skyline
And the lumpish boats on their mirror lake
And their *Greetings from Milwaukee* sign.
The stress and pressure seem too much to take,

Yet they maintain a sunny attitude,
A smile on each injection-molded face;
I'm tempted to admire their fortitude,
But it's not courage if you're glued in place.

Horoscope

The stars are flipping coins and casting lots
To come up with some kind of plan for you;
You'll learn about resolved points in their plots
Through upcoming bolts out of the blue.

In the meantime, you and your free will
Should just continue on your dreamboat course,
Since you will still have several weeks to kill
While life, the snake you're charming, gathers force

To implement some fresh impediment
And let the subtle aftermath unfold.
But what will follow that experiment,
Your next adventure, cannot be foretold,

Because the stars themselves don't even know;
They're making all of this up as they go.

Crop Duster

There's nothing quite like flying your own plane,
Even if it's just a little one.
Up in the air, beneath the blowtorch sun,
Above the sprawling corn and bean domain,
All your humdrum worries slip your brain.
I always hate it when a job is done,
When I've found the right field and made my run
And must descend and walk the Earth again.

I usually deliver pesticide.
I've killed my share of bugs. But I'm for rent
For fertilizer, too, for the same fee.
Depending on who's paying for the ride
I rain down either death or nourishment,
Like a god, but without mystery.

Over the Edge

The wind was strong and at our back all day
So we sped merrily across a sea
Awash with floating patches of debris:
Crates and sea chests bobbing in the spray,
Splintered planks and oars and the odd stray
Capsized lifeboat drifting aimlessly,
All striking our hull lackadaisically
And spinning under on the ricochet.

The boats they sent to stop us have turned back
And there are no birds trailing in our wake;
We sail beyond the maps and charts alone.
And now the waters swirl and skies grow black
And in the distance vast waves rise and break
And we are doomed. If only we had known.

Quo Vadis, Bigfoot?

You're famous, but we never see your face,
Only your blurry form from the rear side
Departing at a brisk bipedal pace,
And no one knows exactly where you hide—

Some say some kind of bent sapling home base
Out in the swamps or woods or hills somewhere,
While others say a cave on a rock face
Or squirrel-like leaf nest high up in the air—

I sometimes dream of disappearing, too,
Of legging it into the woods like you
To find whatever gap you vanish through
To reach someplace completely out of view,

And though I can't run, I hope you still do,
One step ahead of all that's chasing you,
And that they never find your secret lair,
Only a few footprints and tufts of hair.

Insect Collector

There are so many species of insects
You're almost guaranteed to like a few
Because key irresistible aspects
Of their form or behavior enchant you.

I'm drawn to predators that specialize
On an extremely narrow range of prey,
Some star-crossed subgenus of ants or flies
Consumed in a unique, inventive way;

I focus on how they've been modified
To hunt and harvest more effectively,
The body parts reshaped and fortified,
The miniature flamboyant weaponry,

And ponder nature's beautiful detail
And lack of pity, down to this small scale.

Daredevil

I started racing dirt bikes, and soon learned
That what crowds really hope for is a crash,
So being poor from racing, I soon turned
To doing sideshow stunts to earn some cash.

I specialize in high-speed ramp jumps, where
You rocket over large things through the air,
Old cars mostly, but one time a caged bear,
And a retired school bus at the state fair.

The hard part's coming down. I've had some spills
And broken bikes and bones, and been laid up,
But most jumps go fine, and it pays the bills,
So I have not yet had the sense to stop;

I know it takes a heavy toll on me,
But most jobs do that, just less openly.

Ex Organ Donor

I used to check the driver's license box
So they could use my organs for transplants,
Seeing it as a good deed without cost,
Oblivious to any consequence.

It's grim to ponder what might have played out.
Would whoever my heart went to also get
Its bag of tricks and drama? Talk about
A bittersweet, Faustian side effect.

But now I've overshot the age limit
So my heart won't be making any moves.
It's stuck where I can keep an eye on it,
Its situation never to improve,

Scheming as it beats its one-note drum
And matching wits with me for years to come.

Mission Statement

Whiling away time at a muffler shop,
Having examined all the magazines,
I saw a mission statement stapled up
Between the candy bar and coke machines

Which promised best-in-town customer care,
Transparency, respect, and honesty,
Precision diagnostics and repair,
And giving back to the community.

All these praiseworthy goals were news to me,
Things they completely failed to demonstrate
Through absolute, unbroken apathy
Throughout my stopped clock, bug-in-amber wait,

And I achieved a timeless, Zen-like state
While contemplating the entire deal,
Accepting it as part of karmic fate
While knowing the illusion isn't real.

Welder

I planned to buy a used one to set up
In my garage, to teach myself to weld,
Converting the area into a workshop,
Though it's already slightly overfilled.

My father was a welder way back when.
He had a helmet and a toolbox full
Of welding stuff with burn marks on one end,
So I assumed I could skip welding school.

I brought it up, and was abruptly quizzed
On what it cost and what I need it for,
And I lost focus and became confused,
And my welding dream was shown the door

For now, since funding for the deal fell through.
My new plan is to trade something for one
To sidestep budgetary re-review.
I think that's what my father would have done.

5. Smoke and Stone

Matchbook

We twenty brethren formed up like a choir
Were born to feel sandpaper on the face
And burst into a handy ball of fire.
It is a destiny that we embrace.

1 through 3 went for a charcoal grill,
4 and 5 for big candles in jars,
6 and 7 to heat some scented oil,
8 through 10 for gas station cigars,

And so on, until now we three remain,
Seemingly forgotten in a drawer.
Our hearts have turned to stone, yet we maintain
Our focus, our commitment, our desire,

Our certainty that we'll be found someday,
And stricken, and flare up, and burn down to
Spent sticks and ashes, and be thrown away,
Having done what we were meant to do.

Frankenstein

What is it to be human? Is it just
Component parts, arms, legs, a spine, a brain?
The faculty of speech, the use of tools?
Emotions, yearning, sorrow, anger, fear?
I pass each of these tests, and yet remain
Apart from them, a blot upon the earth.

Perhaps humanity comes down to love,
To feel it and to cause it to be felt
In others. If that truly is the case
The matter becomes clearer. I inspire
Not love, but horror, torches, pitchforks, all
Their hideous reflexes of alarm.

A human made me, but could not be made
To love me, to show me that decency.
So I am cast upon the world, a true
Outsider, not of the romantic sort,
No anguished rebel who's misunderstood,
But one beyond the pale, the word made flesh.

I have withdrawn into the arctic wastes
To freeze my passions and to brood upon
My lot, and theirs. My fate is clear enough:
To wander this inhuman emptiness
And die alone, and leave my monstrous corpse
Upon the ice, unburied and unmourned.

I dream of worse for them. They do believe
That their creator loves them, when all facts
Proclaim to me a plain indifference.
Before they die, may each of them perceive
This lonely truth, and feel despair, and see
How little their love means, and think of me.

Lab Rat

My cage is decent, wire mesh, rack-mount style
With built-in feeding tray and drinking spout.
They stack us eight by ten, two racks per aisle.
It's warm and dry. I quit trying to get out.

They feed us pellets, which are excellent,
And the focal point of every day
Is pellet time, the glorious moment
When they pull out your cage and fill your tray.

But there's also tension, fear, and gloom,
Since they instead might grab and carry you
Through the Big Door, to the Other Room.
If that's their plan, there's nothing you can do.

I've seen them come for a specific rat
And also wheel off an entire rack.
They fill their spots with greenhorns, and that's that.
The rats they gather up do not come back.

Nobody knows who or what they are,
Only that they're big and purposeful
And that they feed us. That's about as far
As most rats take the philosophical,

Though you meet deeper thinkers here and there
Who try to puzzle the whole system out,
The Other Room, the clipboards, the stale air.
I listen to them, but remain in doubt;

We're fed here for however long, and then
We're mustered out, abruptly, randomly,
Replaced with new rats, and it starts again.
If there's a point to it, it's hard to see.

Cave Fish

I live in a stream running through a cave
And eat whatever happens to float by:
Insects, worms and larvae, roots and seeds,
Microorganisms, smaller fish,
And leaf litter washed in from outside.

Taste is the only sense that I employ.
When something comes, I touch it with my lips
To know if it is edible or not
And either gulp it down or spit it out.
Thus do I divide my world in two.

Mine is the plainest of existences,
A blind and silent grubbing after food
Face forward in the runoff from above,
A mouth, a stomach, and an appetite
At the dead end of a long food chain.

Yet when something I savor washes down
My swallow reflex nerves all fire at once,
Crackling like fireworks in my mind.
And the water flowing over me
Buoys and soothes me as I float and sway,

And there are other joys. I am content
In that I'm rarely hungry or afraid.
My life is stable and predictable.
And when the stream is rich and running well
There is nothing I would want to change.

But every creature thinks its life is sweet
And strives and struggles to remain alive,
Be it a dominant top predator
That swaggers some lush jungle fearlessly
Or bottom feeder in the bleakest sea.

Flossie

My ear tag has a number, but my name
Is Flossie. I work at a dairy farm
Where every day is pretty much the same:
When they turn the lights on in the barn

We eat some feed, and then are led outside,
Onto the cement slab to be hosed clean,
Then to the milking parlor, where we ride
The continuous rotary milking machine,

Which is our labor, three times every day.
And in between we go to the feed lot
And eat feed from the trough, and sometimes hay,
Which after a good milking hits the spot.

The milker spins slowly. You just step on
And are all prepped and hooked up in a snap,
While right behind, a cow whose round is done
Is being uninstalled to make a gap

For the next cow, one cow off, one on,
And ninety in between them riding steel
In a radially symmetric formation
Like flower petals or spokes on a wheel,

Staring at the hub of the machine,
Where their ninety milk hoses combine
Into an unbroken high-volume stream
Filling trucks and tank cars down the line.

We often talk about our calves, who were
Removed from us a few days after birth
To be prepared, as we once were, for their
Appointed bovine calling on this earth.

We send a sea of milk out every day,
A full quota from every mother cow,
And hope a little of it flows their way.
They all must be getting so big by now.

Rainmaker

Cloud seeding is a pretty good business
Since there is usually a drought somewhere
And farmers who'll pay you to salt the air
With special scientific mystery dust
To cause some rain to magically appear.

The only problem is it doesn't work
Consistently, and often not at all;
You get a few pathetic drops to fall
Or nothing, and you're doubly out of luck
If you did not get paid up front in full.

But once in a great while, I guess by chance,
I send the dust up and the rain comes down
In sheets and buckets, pooling on the ground,
Soaking all the thirsty little plants
And generating good will all around;

When that happens, when by some arcane
Hocus pocus all the stars align,
It drives all the old failures from my mind,
And I feel overjoyed I made it rain
And sad that I can't do it every time.

Toolmaker

In most cases I don't know what they're for;
I get dimensions and a datum scheme
And surface finishes and shank details
And sculpt them out of metal or carbide.
Then I write "fragile" on the shipping box
Although the buyer bought them to cut steel.

I've read that language and the use of tools
Distinguish human beings from animals,
For people unclear on the difference.
Some chimpanzees make tools to use themselves,
But not in bulk to sell for leaves and fruit,
Yet commerce doesn't prove humanity;

Before time, in a world of stone and bone,
A flint axe head was first rubbed smooth with sand,
And people have ground axes ever since,
At times to the exclusion of all else.
So maybe the decisive difference
Is just an inborn urge to sharpen blades.

Safecracker

I took the craft up at an early age.
Back then most jobs were classic steel cube safes
With plain rotary combination locks.
I rolled the dial to feel the tumblers click
With surgeon's fingers and a stethoscope
Or drilled precise holes for my mirrors and hooks.

But all the locks are electronic now,
So that whole art is dead. These days you patch
A gadget into the lock input port
And if you have the right software installed
The door swings open and you grab the loot.
Otherwise you use a diamond saw.

The work is unskilled and inelegant,
Something you could train a chimp to do.
The stars of the show now are the whiz kids
Who make the magic boxes, which are just
Standard locksmith's keypads loaded up
With stolen codes they trade among themselves.

They haven't honed a true and artful skill
Through years of practice, so they lack a sense
Of pride in their profession and themselves.
They dress and stink like bums and have no class,
Yet those of us with real talent are through.
It's tragic what the world is coming to.

Reverse Bird Watching

You can see my house from the highway
But you can't get to it, since it sits
Behind a clump of trees, across a ditch.
So cars and trucks whiz past me all day long
And all I get from them is noise and stench—

Until I gathered up some brush and sticks
And piled them up in one of the back trees
Like a giant nest, and topped it with
A plastic eagle from the garden store—
Where nobody could say what it was for—

And people started stopping by the road,
And word soon spread, which has attracted more,
A steady stream of lookers and parked cars,
Taking pictures, even video.
I'm hoping a tour bus will show up soon.

And while they watch the eagle, I watch them
Through my second-hand binoculars,
Noting all the types and subspecies,
Admiring their plumage and footwork.
I only wish that I could hear their songs.

Merlin

I was not fathered by an incubus,
I'm not a wizard or a sorcerer,
Soothsayer, enchanter, alchemist,
Prophet, Druid priest, or shape-shifter;

I was an orphan raised by well-fed monks
Who lived by swinging censers, ringing bells,
Sprinkling water, selling candle stumps,
And blessing bowed heads with dog Latin spells.

I learned that most people are gullible,
Easily swayed by rumors and portents,
By smoke and cymbals, and vulnerable
To being hoodwinked in their innocence.

I had things well arranged in Camelot,
Having spread the sword-in-the-stone tale
And maneuvered Arthur to the spot
Directly beneath where the crown would fall;

I was his friend and mentor through his reign,
Guiding him through banquets, balls, and jousts,
And keeping books to spare him the mundane
Arithmetic of balancing accounts,

And I affected robes and pointed hats,
Waved wands around and chanted gibberish,
And collected dead toads, newts, and bats,
To the great awe of the populace.

But then Sir Lancelot and Guinevere
Betrayed him, and our dreamy, harmless king
Led his ragtag army off to war
And was killed, destroying everything.

Out of work, with no work to be found
In a kingdom paralyzed with fear,
With talk of evil magic gaining ground
I thought it would be wise to disappear

And left to try my fortunes on the coast,
Where things are, if not better, quieter,
And met a widowed fishwife, and the rest
Is stone-dead history: I married her.

Now life is less regal but no less soft,
Managing the books of the concern,
With ample leisure for strategic thought
On how best to survive on what she earns.

I hear rumors that I've been bewitched,
Imprisoned by the Lady of the Lake,
And similar irritating bumpkin myths,
But I don't plan to set the record straight;

It's in the past, and I must concentrate
On this new mode of living by my wits
And learn its rules, abstruse and intricate,
And a whole new set of magic tricks.

Newton

They closed our college when the plague appeared
And I was ordered home to Lincolnshire.
I was young then, and minded very much
Both Mathematics and Philosophy,
And I could hold thoughts steadily before
My inner eye, the well from which I draw,
For hours, until all was clear to me.

There, aged twenty-two to twenty-four,
I first conceived my System of the World:
The Fluxions and their basic calculus,
The Laws of Motion and of Gravity,
The Optics and the properties of light.
And from these principles I did deduce
The motions of the planets and the seas.

It pleased me, but I told nobody else.
I was concerned to know the Maker's mind,
To glimpse it in His method and design.
I did not care to prove what I had learned
To others, to endure their questioning.
And so for twenty years I kept my peace
And polished and refined my reasoning.

But rumors spread, and others dimly groped,
And at length I gathered all my notes
And wrote my treatise, the *Principia,*
In formal Latin, icy and remote.
It made me a great man, and I was named
President of the Royal Society,
And for income Master of the Mint.

And I am old, and ponder frequently
Upon that boyhood time in Lincolnshire,
Splitting light with prisms in my room,

Thinking about apples and the moon,
When the heavens opened up to me,
Revealing fragments of their mystery,
Wondrous secrets which were mine alone.

Cave Painter

    Lascaux, 16,000 BCE

We come at dawn and enter by torchlight,
Casting wild shadows as we descend
The sloping shaft to reach the hidden site,

A long cave painted past the trail's first bend
With horses, deer, and great bulls in full stride,
All racing headlong toward an unseen end

In two jostling rows on either side.
We slow and pass between without a word,
And hold our torches high and wave them wide;

It is the vision of the running herd,
Painted in the past, over the course
Of the many seasons it recurred;

We are affected by its grace and force,
And want to linger for a longer view,
But our vision is of the red horse

So we continue onward, crouching through
A dwindling passage to emerge inside
A new cave sparsely painted with a few

Half-done horse scenes. We gather and decide
Which sections we will paint, then separate
To organize our lamps and tools beside

Our scattered posts. I trim my lamp and grate
My purest pigment stones and mix the flakes
With drippings from the lamp. I concentrate

On these small tasks, and the deep silence makes
My thoughts and spirit stray and lose their way
Until a sudden rush of hoofbeats breaks

That silence, and in strange light, unlike day,
The red horse comes to where I sit, alone.
His stares into me, and his eyes convey

A fleeting scene of motion, breath, and bone.
Then he rears and gallops out of sight,
And at that moment I touch paint to stone.

Voyager 2

Space is mostly empty. There's some dust,
Not much, and random particles and light
Traversing without purpose, being just
Byproducts of some physics far from sight.

I too traverse it, but not aimlessly;
I have, or had, a mission. I was sent
To tour a string of worlds atypically
Aligned on one side of the sun. I went

Along a carefully computed path
Through space and time, and every year or two,
Through an uncanny miracle of math,
A striking sight would blossom into view—

First Jupiter, the giant, intricate
With swirls of reds and browns, like blowing sands;
Then Saturn, yellow, its elaborate
Ring system split abstrusely into bands;

Then Uranus, fog gray, anonymous,
Its axis skewed by some conjectured blow;
Then Neptune, deep blue, streaked with curious
Linear filaments of methane snow.

At each approach, I trained my instruments
And cameras upon the world at hand
And sent back images and measurements,
Responding to each radioed command

From those who made me. They acknowledged my
Blocks of transmitted data with concise
Check-sum and bit-count messages, which I
Found pleasingly efficient and precise.

But that was years ago. I have flown by
All things of interest, into emptiness,
As was my mission plan. I still supply
Sparse measurements, detailing nothingness,

To those who made me. Sometimes they reply
With terse text strings, telemetry and such,
But there is noise and static now, as I
Am steadily receding out of touch.

I will of course lose all contact someday
And drift in solitude, with no command
To execute or data to relay.
My mission will then terminate, as planned.

I think of that milestone objectively
As something that is certain to occur
Based on my launch date and trajectory,
On time elapsing, as is its nature,

Yet I sometimes find myself pondering
The otherworldly data I returned
To those who made me, and wondering
If they were pleased with me, and what they learned.

About the Author

David Stephenson's poetry has appeared widely in literary journals for many years. His collection *Rhythm and Blues* won the Richard Wilbur Award and was published by the University of Evansville Press in 2008. He was also a six-time finalist for the Howard Nemerov Sonnet Award.

Stephenson is a manufacturing engineer by profession and has worked primarily in the automotive industry. He received B.S. and M.S. degrees in Mechanical Engineering from the Massachusetts Institute of Technology, and a Ph.D. in the same discipline from the University of Wisconsin. He lives in Detroit with his wife, the chemist Maria Clelia Milletti.

www.ingramcontent.com/pod-product-compliance
Lightning Source LLC
Chambersburg PA
CBHW030909170426
43193CB00009BA/792